***

I0786159

Back Away From the Precipice!

The Case for Honesty and Integrity

Authored by

By Paul Redd

Rise Up Books

(www.myriseupbooks.com)

Printed and Distributed by

Amazon Kindle Direct Publishing

Back Away From the Precipice!

The Case for Honesty and Integrity

Contents

Introduction

To be perfectly honest, most people would rather be told that their behavior is acceptable—character flaws and all. They would rather be known for "street smarts"—doing what it takes to get ahead. For many, being totally honest and full of integrity exacts too high a price—to their ego, their time, their wallet, their convenience, their net worth, or to their pride.

It is not my desire in writing this book to paint a picture of negativity and hopelessness regarding our society and our nation, but before I tell it like I think it ought to be, I feel constrained to tell it like it is. In addition, in the writing of this book, I don't wish to imply that there are no people of integrity walking among us. There are great examples, of integrity, of people whose word is their bond. One such individual, Jon M. Huntsman Sr., one of my personal heroes, authored a book entitled, "Winners Never Cheat". When I read his book for the second time, I determined that I want to be known and respected in my circle of influence as a man of integrity like Jon M. Huntsman Sr.

So if you engage in this book, file these ideas, assertions, and questions under "food for thought" or "if the shoe fits . . ." Most of all, as Jiminy Cricket[1] said, "let your conscience be

---

[1] Carlo Lorenzini (pen name, Carlo Collodi (November 24, 1826 – October 26, 1890), *The Adventures of Pinocchio*.

your guide". We can only change our culture one person, one conscience, one family, one household at a time. In the end, I can't change anyone but me and you can't change anyone but you, but we can exert a significant positive influence on those around us. We can lead from the front. Most importantly and primarily, it is in the family that principles of honesty and integrity must be taught. One final thought: What epitaph do you want on your headstone? I'd like mine to be "Man of Integrity, a Lighthouse beside a Troubled Sea".

Prologue

The story is told of the following encounter at sea. Being unable to determine its validity, I use it simply as an illustration to make an important point.

Two battleships assigned to the training squadron had been at sea on maneuvers in heavy weather off the California coast for several days. As night fell, the captain noticed the patchy fog and decided to remain on the bridge. Shortly after dark, the lookout on the wing of the bridge reported, "Light, bearing on the starboard bow." "Is it steady or moving astern?" the captain asked. The lookout replied, "Steady, captain," which meant the battleship was on a collision course with the other ship. The captain called to the signalman, "Signal that ship: You are on a collision course. Advise you alter your course 20 degrees."

Back came the answering signal, "Advisable that you change course 20 degrees." The captain said, "Send another message. I am a senior captain. Change course 20 degrees." "I am a seaman second class," came the reply, "change your course at once." The officer was furious. He spat out, "We are a battleship squadron. Change your course 20 degrees." The flashing light replied, "I am a lighthouse." The squadron changed course.[2]

Whether we face danger from being near the edge at the top of the precipice, or on the water approaching the jagged rocks and shoals at the base of the precipice, the lighthouse plays a critical role. In this instance the lighthouse represents a warning system and an unwavering beacon to keep us from danger. It is akin to an emergency caution to change course before it's too late. This is our society's opportunity to return to honesty and integrity—to a life guided by unchanging principles—before we crash and burn on the rocks at the base of the cliff. If we choose to ignore the warning, at least we do so knowingly.

Acknowledgements

Anyone who has ever authored a book can certify to the many hours spent on outlining, researching, writing, re-writing, and editing. Then there's the cover concept and preparations for marketing and distribution. It is little wonder that those who write must be driven by a passion for their subject matter. Without that passion, we would be "dead in the water".

---

[2] (Proceedings of the U.S. Naval Institute)

It is also my opinion that no one writes in a vacuum. We are all aided by many along the way. Sometimes those who *help* in the work don't even know they are contributing. My attitudes about the subject matter of this book—the need for honesty and integrity—were shaped years ago. My parents: John and Sherrill Redd; a Boy- Scout Leader: Leon Cappell; a church youth leader: Edmund Axford; a university professor: Stephen R. Covey, and many others helped me learn and understand the value of living by these important principles.

I am truly grateful to my niece Emmelyn Redd for the cover drawing of the lighthouse, whose artistic talent belies her young age. She shares her talent freely.

I also wish to express my deep gratitude to my wife, Christine for her editing expertise and input about balance on the presentation of these materials.

"It is discouraging how many people are shocked by honesty and how few by deceit."

Noel Coward[3]

3

http://www.brainyquote.com/quotes/keywords/honesty.html#DGBrTtiHrT8 U3AjH.99

Chapter 1 - Could We Sink Any Lower?

§ § §

What is the greatest ill that afflicts our society? What causes the most pain and suffering? If you could wave a magic wand and have just one social problem go away, which problem would *you* choose? I know what *I* would choose. That is the topic of this book. In the end, you may be inclined to agree. You may even be inclined to help wave the magic wand.

On nearly a daily basis, we read stories of corruption, deceit, subterfuge, reneging on promises, or outright theft, and say to ourselves something like, "Wow, how low can they go?" And you may say, "Hey, wait a minute . . . that doesn't apply to me!" However, without deep introspection and analyzing our own conduct (see the bullet points of "a mostly honest person" later in this chapter and judge for yourself), we may fail to see in ourselves the markings of those same tendencies and proclivities that are the hallmarks of a society that has slipped from its ethical moorings and whose social conscience has become so confused and smothered that it is hardly recognizable. What if news articles were written about acts of dishonesty in our personal, private lives? Could we honestly say we act with *more* integrity than those highlighted in the news media? Is the difference—the gap—only a matter of degrees of the perceived seriousness of the offenses of others? There appears to be no standard of integrity in our society. Honesty is relative, we say. This is a dangerous trend, especially in a society where so many behaviors and transactions are on the "honor system" and where trust plays such a key role. Situational ethics and unscrupulous behavior are commonplace and even highly compensated (until someone is caught!).

This is not intended to be a comprehensive list of all ... but representative of the "secret combinations," even conspiracies at the highest levels of government: state department, FBI, justice department, executive branch, and the IRS top brass.

Consider the example of Matthew Martoma with SAC Capital, a popular hedge fund, who was recently indicted and convicted of trading on insider (non-public) information.

[Matthew] Martoma, SAC Capital Ex-Trader, Gets 9 Years in Prison[4]

Also convicted of trading on non-public information:

"Raj Rajaratnam's remarkable journey from Sri Lanka to the heights of the hedge-fund world to felon ended Thursday when he was sentenced to 11 years in prison, the longest-ever term imposed in an insider-trading case."[5]

---

4 by Matthew Goldstein, New York Times, September 8, 2014 1:02 pm

5 By Susan Pulliam And Chad Bray, October 14, 2011, Wall Street Journal (WSJ)

In fact, there have been dozens of convictions in the past few years of individuals who were involved in insider trading. Anyone in the securities industry knows that insider trading is a big no-no, but many still try to push the envelope and get away with it. I wager that only a small fraction of those who engage in this illegal activity are ever caught.

With that as a backdrop, do you want to be part of the solution or continue to be part of the problem? Do you *really* want to be part of the solution? Honestly? This is a question each person must look deep inside to answer. We all live in our own state of residence, the State of Minnesota, the State of Massachusetts, the State of Oregon, etc. Many also spend significant time in the State of Denial and the state of Delusion. They think they are more honest than they truly are, or don't care about honesty at all. How long can a society exist when its constituents lack a clear moral compass? Our nation, our society appears to be on the brink of collapse-- moral and economic collapse. Unfortunately, the continued weakening moral underpinnings are found at every strata of society, in every community, boardroom, company, government—local, county, state, or federal (and from the lowest to the highest levels). Equally unfortunate is that with the disintegration of the family and lack of moral principles being taught in our homes, the dearth of moral principles among the rising generations bleeds into all of the above organizations and sickens our society like a slow-acting poison that may eventually end in collapse. Eradication of this malady seems nearly impossible, and staving off the collapse of society and the economy seems like an unwinnable challenge. Will you help or hinder in avoiding this seemingly inevitable collapse?

What are we really talking about? How bad is it really? Isn't this indictment just a bit rabid, just a bit fatalistic? You be the judge. Just look at events or trends over the past few years. What do the following have in common?

- The market meltdown from July-2007 through March 2009
- 11,000,000+ illegal immigrants
- Prisons filled to capacity
- Dozens of convictions for Ponzi schemes
- Billions in losses to investors from "Ponzi" schemes
- Acute lack of trust of politicians and between politicians
- High ranking officials and an epidemic of 'regular' people who cheat on their spouses
- Epidemic divorce rates
- Tens of thousands of pages of laws and difficulty enforcing them
- Leaders who fail to fulfill their oath of office
- Huge revenue deficits for state and federal governments
- Tax evasion
- Local government deficits
- Municipal bankruptcies
- High home foreclosure rates
- Insider trading scandals
- Doping convictions among professional athletes
- Trillions in unpaid student loans

- Billions in fraudulent billings to Medicare and Medicaid
- Patent lawsuits over smart phone and tablet technology
- Widespread copyright infringements for books, movies, songs, software
- Epidemic levels of identity theft and security breaches of credit card databases
- Computer hackers stealing consumer and sensitive government information
- Government agency spying and overreach
- Automobile manufacturer emission test cheating

A common thread emerges: each is/was caused by or exacerbated by greed, by lack of integrity, by outright dishonesty, by rationalization, by situational ethics, by political motivations, or by the lack of respect for law or lack of respect for fellow citizens.

Daily headlines from major news sources underscore the pervasiveness of dishonesty, misrepresentation, fraud, deception, graft, misappropriation of public funds, broken campaign promises, and many other forms of the lack of integrity among those in whom the public places their trust. Here are just a few headlines gathered over a sixteen-day period. Some are convictions, others are indictments, but both highlight a deep, ongoing, and pervasive problem.

Recent Headlines:

- "Ex-Detroit mayor convicted of widespread corruption," Reuters, 3-11-2013
- "SEC Accuses Illinois of Securities Fraud," New York Times, 3-11-2013

- "Premium Job Board Sued for Promising Customers Jobs That Don't Exist" PBS 3-12-2013
- "SAC Hit with Record Insider Penalty," Wall Street Journal (hereafter WSJ), Sat/Sun March 16-17, 2013
- "Citigroup agreed to pay $730 million to settle claims that it misled investors in more than four dozen bond and preferred-stock offerings over more than two years, in the second-largest settlement of private securities litigation tied to the financial crisis," WSJ, March 19, 2013
- "A Federal grand jury indicted former Calpers CEO Buenrostro in a long-running "pay-to-play" case involving the retirement system," WSJ, March 19, 2013
- "Obama's pick for labor secretary, Thomas Perez, has come under scrutiny for a deal he helped broker between the government and St. Paul, MN," WSJ, March 19, 2013
- "The FBI said it believes a criminal group based in the mid-Atlantic and New England was behind a $500 million art theft in Boston in 1990," WSJ, March 19, 2013
- "Five ex-officials of Bell, Calif., were convicted on corruption charges related to an overpayment scandal," WSJ, March 21, 2013
- "Federal authorities are weighing insider-trading charges against a younger brother of jailed Galleon founder, Raj Rajaratnam," WSJ, March 21, 2013
- "An informant has led prosecutors to another group of alleged insider traders, including a hedge-fund analyst and the investment chief for Wyoming's retirement system," WSJ, March 27, 2013

- "A federal agency issued a fraud alert about certain commercial entities run by doctors that have proliferated in orthopedic and spine surgery," WSJ, March 27, 2013

That's only the tip of the iceberg. Multiply it by 100 or so and it's still just the tip of the iceberg. And it's a gigantic iceberg.

Government Dishonesty

Two of the greatest threats to our democracy are the failure to enforce our laws and lack of integrity in our government. For 8 long years the Obama administration selectively enforced the laws. The Justice department looked the other way when their cronies decided the laws didn't apply to them—Republicans and Democrats alike—as long as they played along. Government officials aided and abetted rogue nations (our enemies) with arms and money, and 20% of our nation's uranium, with no consequences. Immigration laws were not enforced allowing us to be overrun with millions of illegal immigrants—many of whom don't respect our laws.

We have seen dishonesty in spades with the Hillary Clinton email scandal—where classified emails were kept on a private server in the Clinton's home, exposing it to intrusion by outside hackers. Emails were shared with her assistant Huma Abedin that were subsequently shared with Huma's husband Anthony Weiner, ostensibly to be printed out for Clinton— though Weiner had no security clearance. When questioned, FBI director James Comey answered numerous inquiries in a congressional hearing confirming that Hillary Clinton made false statements with regard to the emails. Prosecution apparently boiled down to intent, according to his reasoning, and he indicated that there was no intent to break the law. Apparently, ignorance of the law *was* an excuse and he declined to prosecute, even though American interests were put at risk and various statutes were broken.

Perhaps the most blatant disregard for principles of honesty and integrity occurred in the run-up to the 2016 presidential election. As of this writing the investigation is still ongoing regarding senior FBI and Justice Department officials colluding to discredit Donald Trump. They also had a backup strategy in case Donald Trump won the election, so that if Trump won the election they would have enough "dirt" on him to have him removed from office either by impeachment or some other means. A fake dossier was created having information about the Trump campaign colluding with the Russians to help win the election, was paid for by the FBI and other anti-Trump organizers. This dossier was used as a basis for obtaining a FISA warrant to surveil the Trump campaign. The arrogance of these government appointees and officials cannot be overstated. Weaponizing of government organizations to overthrow the will of the people is highly illegal-- not to mention it is a direct attack on the principles underlying our Democratic Republic.

Joe Digenova, former US attorney, characterized it this way, "The fundamental principle of this investigation is that a group of senior FBI and DOJ officials in the Obama administration conspired to illegally exonerate Hillary Clinton in the private email scandal to assist her in winning the presidency, and if by chance she lost they had a plan to frame Donald Trump as president in a crime he did not commit. The FBI's and the DOJ's credibility has taken a serious hit."

Another blatant display of dishonesty is by the mainstream media (MSM). Whether or not you like or agree with President Trump, if you look at the MSM's coverage of events involving him, and if you measure time spent on positive, objective reporting, it is about 5-10%. The balance is one-sided, slanted, with key facts missing, and statements taken out of context. The media knows that if you tell a lie often enough soon the public will begin to believe it. One media commentator even declared, "Our job is to control what people think." They are no longer about reporting the news and facts as they stand but are about promulgating a political agenda.

This constant negative biased news being promulgated has given rise to violent protests of all stripes resulting in lawless behavior by groups trying to subvert the current administration and even to overthrow the constitution.

Lawlessness breeds more lawlessness. Look at the violent protests that have occurred since the 2016 election. When people think they won't be held accountable for lawless behavior, there is nothing to stop them from engaging in it. No president is going to change his mind or policies just because violent protesters throw a toddler tantrum. If a law is bad, people should work through proper channels to change it. The only way for our nation to survive and thrive as a free nation, is for its laws to be obeyed or enforced when they are broken and for government authorities to practice integrity. It is time we ALL embraced this principle.

So, let's define the terms that illustrate and describe the basic components of "dishonesty" in its many forms:

Definitions[6]

<u>Disingenuous</u> – Not candid or sincere, typically by pretending that one knows less about something than one really does

<u>Dishonest</u> – Not scrupulous with regard to telling the truth; given to swindling, lying, or fraud; not upright

<u>Untruthful</u> - Not giving the truth; providing untrue facts; lying. Pertaining to falsehood; corrupt; dishonest

<u>False</u> - Untrue; not factual; factually incorrect

<u>Deceitful</u> – Deliberately misleading or cheating

<u>Duplicitous</u> - Given to or marked by deliberate deceptiveness in behavior or speech

<u>Mendacious</u> - Lying, untruthful or dishonest.

<u>Pervasive</u> - Manifested throughout; pervading, permeating, penetrating or affecting everything.

<u>Endemic</u> - Prevalent in a particular area or region

<u>Lie</u> - To give false information intentionally

<u>Deceive</u> - To trick or mislead

<u>Steal</u> - To illegally, or without the owner's permission, take possession of something by surreptitiously taking or carrying it away

<u>Cheat</u> - To violate rules in order to gain advantage from a situation. To be unfaithful to one's spouse or partner.

---

[6] Wicktionary (The online, free, open source dictionary)

<u>Misrepresent</u> - To represent falsely; to inaccurately portray something

<u>Half-truth</u> - A deceptive statement, especially one that is only partly true, is incomplete, (misrepresents reality by telling part of the truth), or alters the time sequence of truths

To use some of these terms in their context:

> The curse of dishonesty in our once great and respected society is pervasive, knows no boundaries, it seems endemic in nature through every region of our country, in nearly every organization, whether private, commercial or public. When people aren't taught from an early age about the value and purpose of honesty in their dealings with their fellow men, or when they discard a once-held value of honesty and integrity because it is inconvenient, unprofitable, unpopular, expensive, or perceived as unnecessary, to lie, deceive, steal, cheat, misrepresent, or tell half-truths is the inevitable result.

Honesty or dishonesty starts at the top. It starts at the top of governments, companies, divisions, departments, and families. Wherever there is leadership, people take their cues from those who lead them. They rationalize their own dishonest behavior by saying, in essence, "If *they* can lie, cheat, or steal, so can I." If the highest authority in the particular sandbox does so, it must be ok. Our leaders set the tone for our collective behavior. Don't misunderstand, I'm not saying we blame our leaders for our own dishonest actions, but where there is a culture of dishonesty, it tends to pervade the whole organization—whatever that organization might be.

That's human nature. It can only change when there is a strong enough incentive, teaching, and example to do so.

Saving face in business, government, social, or family circles also often results in dishonest behavior. Here's a simple solution: If you don't know, say so! 'Thinking on your feet', or 'making something up' seem to be perceived as acceptable even laudable behavior. And if you screw up, blame someone else. If you watch a press conference or a political debate, you'll likely see examples of this. Thinking on your feet is great if answers are founded on truth, but too often they are convenient fabrications. "Fact checking" has become a necessary norm. It comes down to this: if you don't know, say so! There is no shame in saying, "I don't know, but I will find out and get back to you." Obviously, this is just another small facet of a much larger problem. No society can long endure when the majority is dishonest. The whole fabric of a great society is held together by the threads of honesty and integrity. When those threads are removed, the fabric quickly disintegrates. Ethics seem to be severely lacking. Licensed professions such as finance, accounting, law, and medicine, real estate, all require ethics courses as part of continuing education requirements. Maybe governments and other forms of business need training in ethics as well.

If you consider yourself to be truly an honest person, great! **We need more like you.** While perhaps many of us need to make minor tweaks to our character, our light can help illuminate the pathway to integrity for others.

What is the definition of the ideal conditions—*honesty* and *integrity* and their related characteristics?

Honesty: 1: fairness and straightforwardness of conduct
2: adherence to the facts. [7]
Integrity: 1: firm adherence to a code of especially moral or artistic values.[8]
Trustworthy: 1: able to be relied on to do or provide what is needed or right; deserving of trust [9]
Incorruptibility: 1: very honest; incapable of being bribed or morally corrupted [10]

Most people would never consider committing a *serious* crime: burglary, bank robbery, embezzlement, etc.; but how many of us rationalize less serious forms of dishonesty and don't even consider them as being dishonest?

Profile of a "mostly honest" person
- If we get charged too little, we don't say anything, we don't return too much change
- We fudge 5 – 10 mph over the speed limit, roll through stop signs
- Exaggerate the good we do, down play the bad we do
- Take a little more in tax deductions than we deserve
- Lie only about "inconsequential" things—"white lies"

---

[7] Merriam Webster on-line dictionary

[8] Merriam Webster on-line dictionary

[9] Merriam Webster on-line dictionary

[10] Merriam Webster on-line dictionary

- Fudge the truth on an application—job, insurance, credit, etc.
- We only disclose "part of the story" – to protect ourselves, ego, etc.
- In a business deal, or when selling, we exaggerate the "positives" and downplay the "negatives"

If you think honesty and integrity are outmoded and quaint, ask yourself these questions for introspection:

- Would **you** do business with a professional (attorney, CPA, financial advisor) who (if you knew the truth) had been or should have been sanctioned for fraud or misrepresentation?
- Would **you** do business with someone who (if you knew better) would give you less than you paid for or agreed upon?
- Would **you** vote for a public official or candidate for public office if you knew they had no intention of keeping their campaign promises, who fudged on the payment of their taxes, or whose resume or qualifications were falsified?
- Would **you** enter into a contract with a company or individual who (if you knew the truth) had no intention of keeping their contractual obligations?
- Would **you** loan money to someone who had no intention of repaying the loan?

One final note: an additional threats to the fabric of our nation includes teaching our young people revisionist history. Whether a failure to acknowledge the Holocaust or that the Democrats were the party of slavery, history books are being rewritten and "alternate facts" are becoming the story our young people are being taught. This is a very dangerous trend.

Confidence... thrives on honesty, on honor, on the sacredness of obligations, on faithful protection and on unselfish performance. Without them it cannot live.[11]

Franklin D. Roosevelt

---

[11] Franklin D. Roosevelt, First Inaugural Address, Saturday, March 4, 1933

Chapter 2 - How Did We Get Here?

§ § §

Has dishonesty always been with us? In the Holy Bible we read about Adam and Eve's son Cain, who murdered his brother Abel. When asked about his missing brother Cain replied "Am I my brother's keeper?"[12] Cain's disingenuous response shows his motivation to sidestep the question, to hide the truth, to avoid punishment, and save face. Things in our world today haven't changed much.

Some of the motivations for dishonest behavior include: rationalization, greed, expediency, convenience, arrogance, apathy, desperation, etc.

PT Barnum coined the phrase "there's a sucker born every minute". There is a growing segment of our society who makes their living through illegal and dishonest means, often taking advantage of people who don't know enough to avoid them. These activities include the following:

- Sellers of products that are either unsuitable for the purchaser or that have unproven benefits of the benefits advertised (especially prevalent in sales to the elderly or mentally challenged, or uninitiated)
- Those who engage in identity theft
- Those who collect money for a product that doesn't exist

---

[12] Holy Bible, King James Version, Old Testament, Genesis 4:9

- Those who engage in the sale of illegal drugs
- Those who copy or duplicate patented or copyrighted items and sell to others as legitimate
- Those who engage in selling financially fraudulent products, such as Ponzi schemes
- Those who make and distribute counterfeit currencies
- Those who steal and acid wash others' checks
- Those who counterfeit pharmaceuticals
- Those who spew propaganda—lies and falsehoods, certain media outlets, tabloid publishers, both sides of the climate change debate, advocates of changing social structure, certain product manufacturers
- Those who submit fraudulent Medicare claims
- Those who engage in hacking or phishing websites to gain personal information
- "Porch Pirates"—who steal goods just delivered to a residence by a delivery truck
- Those who vote illegally using the name of a deceased person, vote more than once, or vote when they are not citizens of the US

That's just the short list. Dishonest people get increasingly more creative at finding ways of stealing from or defrauding others. It's as if their motto is "do unto others before they do it unto you!"

Very little in terms of behavior in our society happens without its genesis in teaching or lack of teaching. Moral principles are either taught in the home, or by default, or they are taught by society. If parents don't like what society is teaching, it is incumbent on them to teach the desired principles in the home. Those same principles must be reinforced by precept, example, and repetition. If moral principles are not taught to children in the home from an early age, society and their peers will teach some other set of values (good or bad) by default. The saying "the apple doesn't fall far from the tree" has application here. If moral principles are not firmly in place when decision time comes, it will be very easy, and even natural, to adopt an attitude of expediency—whatever the situation demands at the time is the right thing to do—whether it is honest or dishonest.

Closely linked to expediency is rationalization. Even if a person has some degree of ethical orientation—including honesty, it is often seen as more convenient to do the dishonest thing in order to save face, save money, save time, or avoid embarrassment. As previously alluded to, sometimes doing the honest thing is expensive, or time consuming, so one rationalizes that they are just saving money or saving time by doing it in less-than-honest fashion.

One other point: if *conflicting* philosophies to the ones espoused in the home are taught in the schools, then parents need to hold educators responsible or move their children to a school where their moral principles will be reinforced. Sometimes we have to vote with our feet.

A striking recent example of expediency and rationalization leading to dishonesty, is the Bernie Madoff Ponzi scheme (Ponzi scheme: where older investors are paid 'returns' from newer investor inflows). Wikipedia.com provides significant detail about the Madoff Company's Ponzi scheme.   The relevant points are adapted and summarized below:

Bernard Madoff established Bernard L. Madoff Investment Securities, LLC in 1960. His two sons, his brother, Peter, and a niece were employed by the firm until Bernard's and Peter's convictions relating to securities fraud in 2009. Bernard and Peter are currently serving prison terms of 150 and 10 years respectively. Bernard's son Mark committed suicide two years after Bernard's arrest in December 2008.

The day before his arrest, Madoff had admitted to his sons that their "asset management unit was a massive Ponzi scheme . . . describing it as 'one big lie' ". For some reason, the SEC'S previous investigations did not reveal the scheme.

The following year, in March 2009, Madoff entered guilty pleas to 11 federal felonies and admitted his wrong-doing in creating the Ponzi scheme that swindled thousands of trusting investors out of an estimated $18 billion (actual losses) of assets. Madoff indicated the Ponzi scheme began in the 1990's, but investigators placed its beginning back into the 1970's.

Ostensibly, Madoff didn't plan to create the fraud. In his words to Barbara Walters, he said, "Things just got out of hand. I don't believe I'm a bad guy or stupid".[13]

Madoff was able to pull off the scheme because of his visibility and being a respected person on Wall Street.

---

[13] Wikipedia.com

By way of analysis, it is likely that the firm started out as a legitimate investment business and grew to have a reputation to uphold. As they tried to attract new investors, they likely made promises of moderate consistent returns, and when markets didn't perform, especially in a steep market downturn, they resorted to paying those investors with other peoples' money to deliver on their promises. Expediency was the driving force, most certainly brought on by rationalization.[14]

Also problematic was that Madoff's firm acted as *both* the investment manager and custodian. If these two functions had been carried out by independent firms, the scheme wouldn't have been as easy to pull off.

The scheme worked as long as he was able to fund requested withdrawals, thereby maintaining investor confidence and the illusion of positive returns. When the markets tanked in 2008, that appears to have been the catalyst for not being able to fund withdrawal requests; and the fatal blow occurred.

* * *

A more recent example of expediency and rationalization leading to dishonesty or breaking the law is the botched implementation of the Affordable Care Act (also known as

---

[14] "SEC Didn't Act on Madoff Tips-Regulator Was Warned About Possible Fraud as Early as 1999", by Binyamin Appelbaum and David S. Hilzenrath, Washington Post Staff Writers, Tuesday, December 16, 2008

Obamacare). The entire nation was told, "If you like your health insurance plan, you can keep it. If you like your doctor, you can keep him or her." When the administration and congress "found out" that insurance companies would not be allowed (under the ACA) to keep large numbers of people on their "sub-standard" policies and those new plans wouldn't necessarily be accepted by existing doctors, they back pedaled and strong-armed insurance companies to re-allow policies to be reinstated. Ostensibly, the administration and congress knew this would happen before implementation. Policies not meeting Obamacare rules were dropped anyway, in spite of the promise made that "if you like your health insurance plan, you can keep it." (D'Angelo Gore, FactCheck.Org 6:19 p.m. EST November 11, 2013 reported the following in USA Today)

"Americans who purchase such plans on the individual insurance market have been receiving notices that their current plans will no longer be offered after this year, as several news organizations reported in October."[15]

Those notices make it clear that Obama was over-simplifying and over-promising when he kept saying, "if you like your health care plan, you can keep your health care plan."[16]

---

[15] (http://www.cbsnews.com/8301-505263_162-57609534/policy-cancellations-higher-premiums-add-to-frustration-over-obamacare/)
   (http://www.latimes.com/business/la-fi-health-sticker-shock20131027,0,4888906,full.story#axzz2j7tq3Hdn)
   (http://investigations.nbcnews.com/_news/2013/10/29/21222195-obama-administration-knew-millions-could-not-keep-their-health-insurance?lite)
[16] (http://www.factcheck.org/2013/10/realityconfronts- Obamas-false-promise/)

President Obama and key congressional Democrats, including Harry Reid, Dick Durbin, and Patty Murray all echoed the same message.

When the website for signing up for insurance via on-line exchanges was not ready in time, the law was suspended and a legally mandated deadline was extended by executive order. When business owners squeaked about the backlash and loss of jobs due to implementing Obamacare, the deadline for implementing this legally mandated requirement was also extended by executive order. A similar thing happened for the individual mandate to have insurance—it was not going to be enforced because of a legal loophole in the law. This miscalculation undermines the metrics of the published costs to the American people. It also harmed insurers who were told they would have a much larger risk pool from which to insure.

In order to protect our system of government, including the structure of checks and balances against abuses of power, whatever the reasons for the extensions, they shouldn't have been granted without congress' approval. When a law is in place, if it is deemed to be unreasonable or unable to be implemented, the law should be changed by legal channels. If *congress* passed the law, *congress* needs to be tasked with modifying the law. Michael W. McConnell's Op-Ed in the Wall Street Journal, July 9, 2013, supports this argument. He stated the following:

"The administration has yet to offer a legal justification for last week's suspension of the employer mandate. Republican opponents of Obamacare say that the suspension of the employer mandate is such good policy that there's no need to worry about constitutionality, but if the president can dispense with law, and parts of laws, when he disagrees with them, the implications for constitutional government are dire."

When government leaders disregard our constitution and laws that have been passed by duly elected officials, they become a law unto themselves. None of us is safe. This demonstrates a lack of integrity and a lack of respect for those they were elected to serve. They have violated their oath of office. Is that dishonest? Yes. Is it despicable? Yes. Is it treasonous? It could be. The cost of their unethical action is incalculable.

This page intentionally left blank

"There are some things in this life not worth doing. The cost is too high."

(Comment by an unnamed participant in an addiction recovery course)

Chapter 3 – What does it Really Cost?

§ § §

What does dishonest behavior really *cost*? I have a friend who was attending the university who as a poor student, accepted an offer from a supposedly qualified young woman student for a "free" haircut. Later that evening, sporting a less-than attractive haircut, he said "it didn't *cost* me anything, but boy did I pay for it!"

The costs of dishonesty aren't always just dollars and cents—though many have components of monetary loss—but boy can we "pay for it." Costs could also include: loss of trust, loss of credibility or reputation, loss of business, bankruptcy, loss of professional licensure, loss of respect of others or self-respect, loss of friendship, loss of credit standing, loss of a job, loss of a car, house or other financed item, fines or imprisonment (loss of freedom), or even loss of a spouse.

We could go into extensive detail of the measurable costs of dishonest behaviors. At a minimum, we will explore the costs of one area that affects all of us to one degree or another: *retail losses*, including shoplifting, see below. First, let's acknowledge the more hidden costs of *other* behaviors. The following pairs represent the dishonest behavior (1st line) and the resulting costs (2nd line):

Overbilling of medical services *resulting in*
Increased cost of services

Submitting inflated property claims *resulting in*
Increased insurance premiums

Misrepresenting credit worthiness *resulting in*
Foreclosure due to non-payment, increases in interest rates
due to uncollectible debts

Misrepresenting professional credentials *resulting in*
Regulatory fines when the truth is discovered and
embarrassment in the media

Not meeting contractual obligations *resulting in*
Litigation expense and awarded damages

Finally, one of the most recent examples of such behavior is of a large European automaker installing a "by-pass" mechanism to fudge emission testing results *resulting in* the expense of recalling and fixing millions of affected cars, as well as the loss of their good reputation and customer loyalty.

By no means is this an exhaustive list. You can probably think of others—and have certainly been the victim of such cost increases.

Retail Losses
"Inventory loss due to shoplifting, employee or supplier fraud and administrative errors cost U.S. retailers an estimated $44 billion in 2014," according to a survey by the National Trade Federation (NRF) and the University of Florida.

"In 2014, shoplifting accounted for the largest portion of the loss at 38 percent, followed by employee theft at 34.5 percent, administrative and paperwork theft at 16.5 percent, vendor fraud or error at 6.8 percent and unknown loss at 6.1 percent, a candy bar or a pair of jeans," said Bob Moraca, the NRF's vice president of loss prevention.[17]

The Global Retail Theft Barometer released in November 2015, by Checkpoint Systems reports that "Employee theft cost U.S. retailers $16.6 billion in the past year—that's $3 billion more than shoplifting cost them in 2015 and about $10 billion more than vendor and supplier fraud and administrative and non-crime losses cost them combined. Some of the reasons that employees steal include ineffective pre-employment screening, less employee supervision and easy sale of stolen merchandise," the report reveals.[18]

From these statistics, it is easy to see that employee theft and shoplifting led the way in retailer losses. Shoplifting, per se, is a growing social problem with psychological and physiological ramifications. Unfortunately, it crosses the boundaries of age and sex, and is very difficult to prevent. It also affects many different types of retail operations. Key statistics below from The National Association for Shoplifting Prevention reveal insights into the complexity and widespread nature of the problem. (From 2014 data)

---

[17] Reuters, Wednesday, 24 Jun 2015 | 7:26 AM ET

18 By Catey Hill (Marketwatch) Pub. Nov 16, 2015 11:29 a.m. ET, from "Americans rob their employers of $16.6 billion a year, far more than other" countries

- There are approximately 27 million shoplifters (or 1 in 11 people) in our nation today. More than 10 million people have been caught shoplifting in the last five years.
- Approximately 25 percent of shoplifters are kids, 75 percent are adults. 55 percent of adult shoplifters say they started shoplifting in their teens.
- Shoplifters say they are caught an average of only once in every 48 times they steal. They are turned over to the police 50 percent of the time.
- 57 percent of adults and 33 percent of juveniles say it is hard for them to stop shoplifting even after getting caught.
- The excitement generated from "getting away with it" produces a chemical reaction resulting in what shoplifters describe as an incredible "rush" or "high" feeling. Many shoplifters will tell you that this high is their "true reward," rather than the merchandise itself. [19]

The National Association for Shoplifting Prevention also points out:

Shoplifting affects more than the offender. It overburdens the police and the courts, adds to a store's security expenses, costs consumers more for goods, costs communities lost dollars in sales taxes and hurts children and families. [20]

---

19 National Association for Shoplifting Prevention. All rights reserved NASP 225 Broadhollow Road, Suite 400 E – Melville, NY 11747-848-9595

20 National Association for Shoplifting Prevention. All rights reserved NASP 225 Broadhollow Road, Suite 400 E – Melville, NY 11747-848-9595

Let's be clear—the term "shoplifting" is just a nice euphemism for stealing. Stealing is a crime. Stealing is wrong. It sets a bad example for children. It costs way more than the goods that are stolen. For a young adult seeking a career in law, medicine, public accounting, or financial advising, a conviction for shoplifting or theft from an employer may disqualify them from getting a professional license. By the same token, stealing from an employer (time, money, or goods) is a crime. It is wrong. No one is entitled to goods they didn't pay for.

One other area of stealing—taking that which doesn't belong to us without paying for it—is "piracy". This involves obtaining copies of videos, music, and books, etc. without making proper payment. It has become too easy to bypass copy protection technology to make copies of these creations and share them with others. The creators of these works have spent considerable time and resources to bring their work product to market, not to mention the cost of developing their craft to be able to produce such work. They deserve to be paid for their efforts. Obtaining copies of their works through "the backdoor" is stealing. It bypasses formal channels through which their products are sold so they can be paid for their work. The cost of piracy is difficult to measure, but it is likely very significant.

Sharing your password to paid subscriptions like video and music streaming services and on-line news services is another form of piracy, and in direct violation of the terms and conditions of your subscription agreement.

Whatever the reasons one might give for gaining access to copyrighted media or content without proper payment, wouldn't hold up in a court of law. Taking the easy way out—cheating the system—and then getting caught and prosecuted is often the most expensive. One must take into account the monetary and non-monetary costs in weighing such a decision. Our decisions, which may seem to only affect us personally, are rarely made in a vacuum. There are almost always other victims bearing the brunt of our dishonest actions.

This page intentionally left blank

I believe fundamental honesty is
the keystone of business.

Harvey S. Firestone [21]

---

[21] Read more at
http://www.brainyquote.com/quotes/keywords/honesty_2.html#7XOP6gPY
DIG3WFQu.99

Chapter 4 - Is it Personal or is It Just Business?

§ § §

Some individuals seem to be able to apply a different standard to business dealings than to personal dealings—saying in essence, it's just business—it's not personal. And being able to separate the two somehow makes it ok?

It's not personal?

Dishonesty is always personal. It affects the person who commits it. It affects the person to whom the dishonest act is done or who is ultimately affected by it. When a dishonest act is committed on us, it is always personal because it affects us personally. Whether it is being robbed, cheated, having our identity stolen, given less than we bargained for, given something different than we contracted for; whatever it is, we feel violated, less safe, less trusting, and more on guard and cynical. We become very unlikely to continue doing business with the person or company represented by the one who perpetrated the act upon us.

Consider a political candidate who comes to our door, asks our opinions, then makes a statement that when they are in office, they will do specific things relating to our concerns. Then after they are elected, they proceed to do just the opposite of what they promised us. Would you feel violated? Would you trust them? Would you vote for them when they are up for re-election? Would their violation of your trust feel personal?

Also consider a person who is cheating or caught cheating on their spouse. Can you think of a more personal offense? Can one even begin to measure the damage to the spouse, children, extended family, friendships, or to social or business standing?

Reflect on damage to a person's reputation by spurious gossip or by outright false accusation. Reputations are routinely damaged by gossip. Perhaps having the perpetrator rip open a pillow filled with feathers and requiring them to recover every feather might be a good learning experience. The ripple effect of such gossip can be enormous.

It's just business, it's not personal

There is no such thing as a "corporate conscience" or an "honest organization". The integrity of an organization rises and falls on the degree of ethical conduct and the attitudes of the *individuals* within the organization. Also, be very certain that the culture of ethics in the firm starts at the top. If corporate officers and directors turn a blind eye to ethical or other violations, you can be certain that such an attitude will eventually permeate the entire organization. Just like water, these things tend to follow the path of least resistance. In fact, if one can rationalize dishonest acts in their personal life, it will be much easier to rationalize them in their business dealings and vice versa.

An honest organization is led by honest people and staffed by honest people. This culture is formed at the top and continues through to the rank and file. In such a company, honest conduct is expected, and everyone knows it. If people don't lie, they don't have to remember what they said. Documenting conversations never hurts, though, because it helps remind us of our commitments and those made by other parties. A company of honest people never has to worry about being on the wrong side of the law, because they never go there. The following might describe the profile of an honest company.

- They offer good products or services for a reasonable price—they offer value
- They honor guarantees
- They respond appropriately and fairly to customer inquiries
- They are good citizens in the community
- Press releases are accurate and truthful
- There is transparency in governance—they disclose what they are doing
- They don't "cook the books;" they provide transparency of accounting records
- They honor contracts into which they enter, and their negotiations are win-win
- They don't mislead shareholders or potential investors
- They pay taxes owed

***

One of the biggest sources of stress we can experience is from the discomfort we feel when our *conduct* isn't congruent with our *conscience*. We can't be a conniving, back-stabbing, or a 'throw-others-under-the-bus' type of person at work and expect that conduct not to spill over into our personal and family life. Yes, it's personal and not just business!

***

One well-known example of one whose personal and business lives were congruent was Abraham Lincoln:

Consider the following quotes about Abraham Lincoln. I am confident in saying that those being quoted or paraphrased had no incentive to speak good (or ill) of the president. These quotes appear to be candid observations by people who spent time with "Honest Abe", as well as by Lincoln himself.

As Lincoln was garnering support for a presidential run, Edward Bates, one of Mr. Lincoln's former rivals, said this of Lincoln: "I give my opinion freely in favor of Mr. Lincoln . . . If Mr. Lincoln should be elected, coming in as a new man . . . he may render great service to his country . . . He can march straight forward in the discharge of his duties, guided by his own good judgement and honest purposes, without any necessity to temporize with established abuses, to wink at the delinquencies of old party friends . . . in short, he can be an honest and bold reformer . . ."[22]

Frederick Douglass describes his first meeting with President Lincoln. He recalled that he had "never seen a more transparent countenance." He could discern "at a glance the justice of the popular estimate of the President's qualities expressed in the prefix 'honest' to the name of Abraham Lincoln"[23]

In speaking of his commitment to pass the Emancipation Proclamation, Lincoln stated, "It cannot be retracted, any more than the dead can be brought to life . . . the promise being made, must be kept."[24]

Would that we had millions like Abe who prized integrity, who were true to their word, their principles and commitments, who didn't bend because of political expediency or other inconvenient pressures.

***

Now let's explore a few ideas about professional ethics. As mentioned in Chapter 1, most "professionals", by definition,

---

[22] The American Party Battle: election campaign pamphlets, 1828-1876; Volume 2; Volumes 1854-1878

[23] "Abraham Lincoln": Frederick Douglass to George L. Stearns, August 12, 1863, (photocopy), container 53, Papers of Frederick Douglass, Manuscript Division, Library of Congress

[24] Abraham Lincoln to James Conkling, August 26, 1863, in Collected Works of Abraham Lincoln , Volume VI, pp 407 - 410

have to be licensed. Periodic continuing education courses are required to maintain a license. These courses almost always include ethics education. In spite of receiving ethics training, I have witnessed licensed professionals whose "good" ethical standards are scarcely discernible. By the same token, there are many that practice a high standard of ethics in their business dealings. I am grateful to have known many such professionals. In my 16 years in a licensed profession, I have developed some practices, witnessed those of others, and made some observations that may be helpful:

- Clients are the lifeblood of your business. When you treat them fairly and honestly, they will work with you for many years. They will also refer family members and friends to you.
- Be dependable. Keep appointments and be punctual. When clients have to wait a long time in a waiting area to see you, because you are running late, they lose respect for you. If you let them know you are running late, they usually understand.
- Don't kill the goose that lays the golden egg. Making a short term profit at the expense of a client's well-being will kill the goose.
- Never give unsuitable recommendations based on limited information you may have. If you are unsure about whether a certain course of action is suitable, gather more information—ask more questions—find out the client's goals in seeking your services.
- If they ask you a question you aren't sure how to answer, offer to do further research and get back to them.

- Keep commitments. If you say you will do something, do it. Give an estimated time frame. Follow up if you are delayed. Wherever possible, under promise and over deliver.
- Give the client enough information to make an intelligent decision.
- Tell the truth. Explain the positives and negatives of a potential course of action. Don't promise what you can't deliver.

Government ethics have long been a concern for many "looking in from the outside." We have become frustrated with what we perceive as abuses of power, money, and public trust. Again, there are many that practice a high standard of ethics in their dealings in government roles. For those of whom this is true, we applaud you. The following observations and guidelines apply especially to elected officials and the people they appoint.

- You work for us-- be accountable.
- Your Presidential office, U.S. Senate seat or House of Representatives seat is a temporary assignment, not a career. We can un-elect you.
- Don't spend money we don't have. American households have to work within a budget. *We* can't print 'unlimited' money. Printing money debases our currency.
- Use the tax and fee revenue you collect from us wisely. Be frugal. We have to! Uncover and eliminate waste.
- No more pork without our approval.

- Vote yours and *our* conscience. You have an obligation to your constituents—we who elected you.
- Fight for what is right, not for what is expedient.
- No more closed-door, single-party votes. The other party deserves to give input.
- Uphold the U.S. Constitution. You took an oath of office and pledged to do so.
- When we write to you with our deep concerns, don't send us a "pat-on-the-head" form letter saying thanks for writing or ignore our communication altogether. It sends the message that our concerns are not important and makes us feel that we have no voice.
- We feel like second-class citizens when you pass laws you don't subject yourselves to. You are not above the law. Play fair!
- Don't make promises you don't intend to keep—whether seeking office or in office.
- Be transparent. This is our country too. Your decisions aren't made in a vacuum.
- Never forget: ours is a government "by the people, for the people, and of the people"!

Need we say more?

This page intentionally left blank

Honesty is not a value shared by all societies. In some Eastern subcultures there is a saying: "Any fool can tell the truth. It requires a man of some sense to lie well." The society espousing this idea suffers abject poverty above others.

Daniel M. Keeran, "If There Is No God"[25]

---

[25] Read more at http://www.notable-quotes.com/h/honesty_quotes

Chapter 5 – What if Nothing Changes?

§ § §

George Santayana observed, "Those who cannot remember the past are condemned to repeat it." [26]

If we are foolish enough to ignore the past, we will commit similar mistakes to those that caused the fall of great empires and societies. If we fail to implement solutions, such as those set forth in the previous and next chapter, we face continuing decline towards the final disintegration of all we hold dear.

The timing of the final disintegration of our society into lawlessness or anarchy is uncertain for us. If nothing changes to reverse the course of the ills we have discussed, it is *inevitable*. It will be the proverbial "death by a thousand cuts". Again, the law of the harvest is relevant here. Look at each great society from our world's history that no longer exists. Thus the invitation in the title of this book, **Back Away From the Precipice!** They all followed the same path. When standards of honesty and morality were abandoned, the beneficial society ceased to exist. Perhaps religion or a system of moral principles has a place after all. At least most religions teach a system of morals, as illustrated in the previous chapter. There are those persons who exercise their constitutional right not to believe in God. But you don't have

---

[26] Read more at http://www.notable-quotes.com/h/honesty_quotes, George Santayana, philosopher, essayist, and novelist (16 December 1863 in Madrid, Spain – 26 September 1952 in Rome, Italy)

to be a religious person to believe in the value of honesty and morality. Such morals are the glue that holds the society together. This has been proven time and time again throughout the history of the world. Are there societies today that are further down the road than others to becoming a "failed state"? Are there societies where civility is declining?

John Locke (1632 – 1704), influenced the thinking of several of the American revolutionaries. His writings about civil society are summarized in the following paragraphs.

"Therefore, Locke set forth two treaties on government with reciprocal obligations. In the first treaty, people submit themselves to the common public authority. This authority has the power to enact and maintain laws. The second treaty contains the limitations of authority, i.e., the state has no power to threaten the basic rights of human beings. As far as Locke was concerned, the basic rights of human beings are the preservation of life, liberty and property. Moreover, he held that the state must operate within the bounds of civil and natural laws." [27]

". . . Locke had set forth a system, in which peaceful coexistence among human beings could be ensured through social pacts or contracts. They considered civil society as a community that maintained civil life, the realm where civic virtues and rights were derived from natural laws. However, they did not hold that civil society was a separate realm from the state. Rather, they underlined the co-existence of the

---

[27] Wikipedia.com

state and civil society. The systematic approaches of Hobbes and Locke (in their analysis of social relations) were largely influenced by the experiences in their period." [28]

This thinking, upon which our government is based, is still valid four centuries later. However the concept of civil society is thought to be originally Roman and was given voice by Cicero. The ideal of a civil society is many centuries old, and yet many nations in our modern world seem to have ignored the lessons of the past. The trouble often begins, and civility is upended, when government and law enforcement officials become a "law unto themselves". Their "cooperation" (which takes many forms) can be bought by criminals, and the self-defeating cycle is hastened. Then it's every man or woman for themselves, just out of self-preservation.

More well-known modern-day examples of countries where corruption is deeply rooted in society are found in Latin America, the Middle East, Africa, the former Soviet Union, and Southeast Asia. Many of the countries plagued by corruption have identified and prosecuted offenders. The U.S. has its own problems with corruption, though perhaps not to the degree of some of these foreign countries. Possibly the corruptions here are more subtle and difficult to detect. Often this corruption takes the form of law enforcement officers and government officials being "on the take" to "look the other way" when organized crime occurs. The typical offenders include drug cartels and mafia-like organizations.

---

[28] Wikipedia.com

Some of our neighbors to the south are currently combatting drug cartels, whose members have murdered hundreds, if not thousands, of innocent citizens as well as rival drug gang members.

If nothing changes to stem corruption and the flow of illicit drugs and arms into the U.S., we may end up on the brink of anarchy where laws aren't being sufficiently enforced as in many of the areas of the world mentioned above. When the laws aren't enforced, a power vacuum is created, and organized crime takes over to fill the vacuum.

Whose job is it to take action against these threats? I would submit that anyone who cares about the long-term viability of this nation, for the good of present and future generations, has the responsibility to work toward real and achievable solutions.

Edmund Burke noted, "The only thing necessary for the **triumph** of **evil** is for good men to do nothing."[29]

---

[29] BrainyQuote.com

This page intentionally left blank

Honesty is a person's most valuable asset. His or her good name, good reputation, and good word depend on the individual's quality of honesty. A business that operates under the principles of profound honesty is elevated within the community. It is respected and treasured. The absence of honesty is a liability to an individual or business.

James H. Merkel & Abdul Wahad Al-Falaij, *"On the Art of Business"*[30]

---

30 Read more at http://www.notable-quotes.com/h/honesty_quotes

Chapter 6 – Is There a Solution?

§ § §

Perhaps the first step in identifying solutions is admitting there is a problem. Let's call a spade a spade. Whether you espouse any religion or system of moral principles, or none at all, you have to recognize that to lie, cheat, steal, misrepresent, tell half-truths, mislead, break promises and commitments, misappropriate funds or other resources, require bribe money or pay-to-play, embezzle, extort, or anything related to the same is WRONG. Too many are the victims of short-term thinking. Those who deal dishonestly want what they want and they want it now, regardless of the means or the consequences of achieving their desire. No beneficial society can long endure under those conditions. A society that embraces or turns a blind eye to dishonest behavior will ultimately fail. Granted, there are occasionally areas that require judgment calls when issues are less than clear, but in most cases there is a bright line between ethical behavior and outright dishonesty. The law of the harvest says that that which one sows, he will also reap.[31] There will be consequences for dishonest behavior—unfortunately not always immediately—to the perpetrator. As indicated earlier, *we* see the consequences every day in increased costs of doing business, increases in insurance premiums, increases in fees, increases in mistrust, lost credibility, failed organizations, failed families, etc.

---

[31] Bible- King James Version 1611, Job 4:8

It would be refreshing to see a corporate organization or a governmental entity implement a culture of immediate dismissal for dishonesty. Not just a hand slapping or temporary suspension, once guilt has been established through due process. Those who are in the public trust have no business being in a position of public trust when they act without integrity—when no one can trust them. As a society, we should not allow it. If we can elect them, we can "un-elect" them and if they are appointed, then they can be un-appointed.

You may recall in the motion picture "Remember the Titans,"[32] a conversation between one of the players, Junius, and team captain, Gary: Gary was lamenting the division between the two races on the team and that the players' performance was reflected in the divisiveness. Junius looked at Gary and stated tersely, "attitude reflects leadership". If our leaders attitudes reflect less-than-ethical or unhealthy philosophies about achieving society's desires, then perhaps a change in attitude or leaders is in order. If the attitudes of many in our society about ethical and honest behavior are less than desirable, changes are also in order.

Granted, there may be instances of someone breaks the law without being aware of it. Because of the voluminous pages that make up the federal legal code, the tax code (78,000 pages), and state and municipal codes, there is great potential

---

[32] Walt Disney Pictures, 2000

for unknowingly breaking a law. Most people however know enough of basic laws to avoid trouble.

Sometimes, I feel like I would like to shout from the housetops this message to those who knowingly engage in dishonest or unethical behavior: "If you don't like this country, then leave! If you are incapable of abiding by the laws, then get out—and don't let the door hit you on the way out! If you are unwilling to act with integrity, for the good of society then go somewhere else and be a burden on them! We have enough problems to deal with without your adding to them by your lying, cheating, stealing, misrepresenting, deceiving, taking undue advantage, and all other forms of law breaking." Chapter 7 addresses additional possible solutions to those found in this chapter.

There are those whom many of us would like to see leave and never return—career criminals among them. Our current laws don't allow for them to be forced to leave our country. This is unlike Great Britain and other colonial nations were known to do in the 18th and 19th centuries to separate criminals from their general societies by sending them to penal colonies in distant lands.[33] There are also those who are here illegally who aren't citizens, who may or may not be otherwise law-abiding. It begs the question, if they willingly disregard our immigration laws and requirements and knowingly game the system, how can we trust them to obey the other laws that govern our society? Additionally, why are there so many

---

[33] Wikipedia.com—see "penal colonies"

citizens that promote amnesty for those who have broken our laws with impunity? Where has respect for law and order gone?

One of the most serious problems in our country—where it is obvious that the law has been broken—is illegal immigration. This amounts to cheating the system to enter our doors—to disregard our laws and demand rights and privileges they haven't earned or shouldn't have. There are many schools of thought regarding illegal immigration. For many this is a politically sensitive topic. When illegal immigration is discussed, and labelled as such, it should be self-evident that the key issue is *it is illegal*! Those who are here illegally have violated the law or are offspring of those who have. We all recognize that there are conditions that drive people to leave their native countries in search of a better life. But they need to gain entry to the United States legally. They need to apply for legal immigration status. The laws exist to protect the interests of those who are here *legally*—from economic harm, bodily harm, harm to property, etc. Government leaders who ignore this reality and those who support them undermine the rights and protections to which the law-abiding citizens of our nation are entitled.

Citizens in good standing have specific rights granted by the Constitution. Also, privileges are granted to citizens who meet certain requirements—such as those required to drive, to vote, and to use public services, schools, public facilities and infrastructure, as well as to have fire and police protection. When a person is convicted of a felony and is incarcerated, they lose personal freedoms, as well as the right to vote and access to certain privileges. One of these privileges is that law-abiding citizens can come and go at will. If someone has a valid passport, they can legally enter other countries. There is a tacit understanding that they will obey the laws of the country they are entering. As long as border and immigration officials allow entry, they are entitled to stay for a limited time as a guest. If they exceed the specified time, they are there illegally and have violated the law and can be prosecuted. They will likely be forced to leave. In essence, they are now "trespassing". If they cross the border without valid documentation, they are likewise trespassing.

When a person from another country crosses our border without valid documents, they are "breaking and entering" so to speak. They are here without permission. They are trespassing. Consider this question: what is the difference between a person entering our country illegally and someone who "breaks into and enters" someone's home and is there without the property owner's permission? Are they not trespassing? Can they not be prosecuted?

The same logic applies to those who enter our country illegally—they can be prosecuted; they shouldn't be granted rights and privileges that our citizens or those who enter our country legally have. There may need to be reasonable requirements that allow illegal immigrants to "make amends", to "set the record straight", to provide reasonable restitution and fund the required processes to gain lawful entry and citizenship.

Fulfilling the following requirements would help demonstrate the applicant's desire and ability to become a law-abiding and contributing citizen of the United States:

- Step forward and acknowledge illegal status within 30 days of a public announcement of a documentation initiative. Otherwise, be deported if caught and pay applicable fines
- Provide proof of payment of taxes over a mandated period of time
- Provide proof of sufficient employment and income
- Obtain sponsorships from U.S. citizens
- Provide character witnesses
- Pay for fingerprinting and pass a background check
- Pay fines and attend immigration court funded by fines and presenting to the court the above documentation and witnesses
- Attend immigration training and pass a competency test—in English—also funded by fines
- Pay taxes on income that hasn't been taxed— stretching back over a reasonable period
- Obtain temporary legally issued ID and temporary Social Security number equivalent until legal status is obtained
- Any person with a felony record or with certain serious misdemeanor convictions can be deported

Let's acknowledge that for those who find themselves on the wrong side of the law—whether or not they have been known, caught and convicted—that's why we have laws and punishments. Unfortunately, most find a way to rationalize dishonest behavior, and therefore don't recognize it as dishonest at all. Expediency rules the day. Unfortunately, most crime goes un-convicted and unpunished. Most abuses of our fellowmen through any form dishonesty are not made right. Think about it—if you had a choice of living in a perfectly honest society where you could leave your doors unlocked, not have to password protect everything of value, and where one's word or handshake was his or her bond, would you rather live there or in our present here and now?

If the USA is ever to achieve the stature of a great society, it will take more than technological innovation, more than quality education available to all who want it, more than properly balanced government and adherence to the U.S. Constitution, more than upgraded infrastructure, more than racial equality, more than a general economic prosperity. In fact, many of these conditions will not be realized unless we individually and collectively embrace a culture of honesty and integrity. It is a chicken or egg thing—which comes first?

All major world religions teach a system of moral principles or commandments that help shape the culture of their respective countries and their adherents. Examples of these are found in the Holy Bible, the Quran/Al-Hadith, the Torah, in the writings of Buddha, and in the teachings of Shintoism.

"Lying lips [are an] abomination to the LORD: but they that deal truly [are] his delight." [34]

---

[34] Bible- King James Version 1611, Proverbs 12:22

"Better [is] the poor that walketh in his integrity, than [he that is] perverse in his lips, and is a fool." [35]

"These six [things] doth the Lord hate: yea, seven [are] an abomination unto him: . . . A false witness that speaketh lies; and him that soweth discord among brethren." [36]

Woe unto those who give short measure, those who, when they are to receive their due from people, demand that it be given in full but when they have to measure or weigh whatever they owe to others, give less than what is due. Do they not know that they are bound to be raised from the dead (and called to account) on an awesome Day, the Day when all men shall stand before the Sustainer of all the worlds?" [37]

"Truthfulness leads to righteousness, and righteousness leads to Paradise. In addition, a man keeps on telling the truth until he becomes a truthful person. Falsehood leads to wickedness and evil-doing, and wickedness leads to the (Hell) Fire, and a man may keep on telling lies till he is written before God, as a liar." [38]

The Torah says: "Distance yourself from words of falsehood." This is the only sin regarding from which the Torah warns us to "distance" ourselves. [39]

---

[35] Bible- King James Version 1611, Proverbs 19:1

[36] Bible- King James Version 1611, Proverbs 6:16-20

[37] Quran 83:1-6

[38] Saheeh Al-Bukharom (From "Al-Hadith, Analysis and an Overview"- The Hadith has come to supplement the Holy Qur'an as a source of the Islamic religious law. The Hadith is the second pillar after the Qur'an upon which every Muslim rests his faith. Hadith consists of Mat'n and Isnad. Mat'n means the text of the Hadith, while Isnad means the chain of transmitters to that Hadith.)

[39] Parshat Toldot by Aryeh Citron

The Buddha taught complete honesty, with the extra instruction that "everything a person says should be truthful and helpful." [40]

"Peacefulness, self-control, austerity, purity, tolerance, **honesty**, knowledge, wisdom and religiousness – these are the natural qualities by which the Brahmans work" [41]

"Shinto today is a term that applies to the religion of public shrines devoted to . . . dimension of Shinto, focusing on sincerity (makoto), **honesty** (tadashii) and purity." [42]

Reportedly, approximately 80% of the U.S. population believes in God, although with interpretational differences; let's pose a few pointed questions about what most people believe about God.

- Does God keep His promises? Always?
- What if He didn't keep His promises? Can He be arbitrary or capricious and still maintain the trust, admiration, respect of those who worship and believe in Him?
- Could *you* worship a God who didn't keep His promises?

---

[40] Sylvia Boorstein

[41] (Bhagavad-gita 18.42) (The *Bhagavad Gita* . . . referred to as simply the Gita, is a 700-verse Hindu scripture in Sanskrit that is part of the Hindu epic *Mahabharata*.-- Wikipedia) (*emphasis added*)

[42] The American Academy of Religion 44.3 (1976), 547-561 in JSTOR; quote p. (emphasis added)

Do we keep our promises? Can we be trusted? Are we dependable? Is our integrity unquestionable? **If not . . .**

STOP IT!

Have some among us received a blunt-force trauma to the head? Have we been taking delusion medication? These things are not ok!!

- Stop applying for benefits you know you don't qualify for
- Stop applying for loans based on false or exaggerated information—assets, income, or employment
- Stop taking tax deductions you don't deserve
- Stop submitting reimbursements for claims for inflated values or for things that you didn't own
- Stop making promises you know you won't keep—campaign, business, personal promises, or whatever
- Stop asking for discounts you aren't entitled to (honest haggling is ok!)
- Stop inflating your resume
- Stop fudging your time card
- Stop inflating appraisals
- Stop stealing from your employer (goods, time, supplies, faxing, use of company vehicle etc.) If your employment contract says you may use incidental supplies for personal use, ok, be fair; but if not, hands off!
- Stop checking social media accounts on company time
- Stop walking out of stores without paying for goods.

- Stop submitting requests for reimbursements to insurance companies, Medicare, or Medicaid that are fraudulent or overstated
- Stop pirating videos, music, books, music, video streaming services, and counterfeiting goods
- Stop saying it needs fixing when it doesn't, and then charging a customer for an unneeded repair
- Stop misrepresenting products you sell
- Stop making fraudulent or misleading statements
- Stop misrepresenting your experience, your credentials, and your skills to those who need to trust you
- Stop misappropriating public funds under your care
- Stop rationalizing that you deserve more than you are contractually allowed to receive
- Stop window dressing your corporate books to create a false impression
- Stop downplaying known risks to your company's stock to appease shareholders or attract new ones
- Stop taking compensation you don't deserve when your company performs poorly
- Stop professing to believe in certain principles and values while you act in a contrary manner
- Stop publishing lies in the press or reporting in an unbalanced or deceptive manner
- Stop stealing hotel towels and other goods you didn't pay for

* * *

To quote a wise religious leader, Elder Sheldon F. Child, "Honesty and integrity are not old-fashioned principles. They are just as viable in today's world. We have been taught . . . that:

- When we say we will do something, we do it.
- When we make a commitment, we honor it.
- When we are given a calling, we fulfill it.
- When we borrow something, we return it.
- When we have a financial obligation, we pay it.
- When we enter into an agreement, we keep it."[43]

Commit to being a person of unshakeable integrity. Decide to keep all of your commitments. Take full responsibility for your actions. Teach your children and others over whom you have stewardship to keep their commitments to you and others. Determine the consequences together for not keeping the commitment when you enter into an agreement, and ask the person if they are willing to accept the consequences for not doing so. The benefits of unshakable integrity are that people will trust you and know they can depend on you. You will also gain self-confidence and self-esteem from keeping your commitments.

---

[43] Ensign Magazine, May 1997

This page intentionally left blank

The man who is so conscious of the rectitude of his intentions as to be willing to open his bosom to the inspection of the world, is already in possession of one of the strongest pillars of a decided character. The course of such a man will be firm and steady, because he has nothing to fear from the world, and is sure of the approbation and support of Heaven.

William Wirt, speech at Rutgers College, Jul. 20, 1830[44]

---

[44] Notablequotes.com

Chapter 7 – Utopia Revisited

§ § §

Unfortunately, it was much easier finding fodder that supported the thesis of this book relating to pervasive dishonesty in our society than it was finding examples of honesty or integrity. How sad. What a sobering indictment of our culture.

However, there is a pattern—based on tried and true principles that if practiced would greatly increase our society's chances of survival.

In his landmark bestseller, Principle Centered Leadership, the celebrated management consultant, Dr. Stephen R. Covey, taught about **principles** and the value of leading, living and working—governing our lives—by principles. Doing so keeps us from being tossed about by the shifting waves of popular opinion and expediency. Leadership, obviously implied by the title, occurs in our own personal lives, in families, and in organizations of all types and sizes. Consider the following excerpt—valuable insights shared in his book:

"Principles are self-evident, self-validating natural laws. They don't change or shift. They provide "true-north" direction to our lives when navigating the "streams" of our environments . . . Principles apply at all times and in all places . . . At the root of societal declines are foolish practices that represent violations of correct principles . .

. we cannot violate these laws with impunity . . . Principles . . . are objective and external."[45]

Moral principles, as previously demonstrated, form the foundational doctrines of all the world's major religions. There are commonalities and intersections of those principles across the religions. Their founders would categorically state that such principles came from a divine source—higher than the mind of mere mortal man or woman.

Living by principles, as opposed to living by shifting societal norms, provides an anchor—or a polar star—an indication of "true-north" as Dr. Covey stated. They become *who we are*, not just *what we do*. The emotional and spiritual constancy provided by principle-centered living affords a foundation for stable and sustainable relationships in families, friendships, businesses, governments, and in any other walk of life. Otherwise, we can be tossed about like a ship without a rudder, when life's storms and challenges arise, whether they are inter-personal, work-related, political, or otherwise.

This concept of "being" (who we *are*, nor just what we *do*) is perhaps the spiritual or moral equivalent of being "in the zone" as described by great performers in sports, music, art, oratory or any other skill-based endeavor. Such a performer reaches a point at which they don't have to think through— step-by-step—each next action. It's almost as if they are on auto-pilot. The "performance" they are engaged in is just a

---

[45] Stephen R. Covey, "Principle Centered Leadership", Simon and Schuster, Inc., 1990, p. 14

part of who they are, whatever skill they employ. They "own" it. You see this time and time again in Olympic performances.

So when someone is confronted with a situation in which there is a potential for making a dishonest choice, as opposed to a choice governed by correct principles—a true case of wrong versus right—they make the right or moral choice without considering other options. For example, a friend of mine, if she isn't charged for something she finds in her grocery bag upon returning home, will return to the store to pay for it. It isn't up for discussion or debate. She goes back to set things right. That's just *who she is*. Those are principles of honesty and integrity she lives by.

The Latin derivation of the word principle is *principium*[46]— literally, that which is first. This definition would corroborate that principles, as Dr. Covey stated, are indeed *foundational, self-evident, and self-validating, proven*, and that they are indeed *based on natural laws*. They come first; they govern all beneficial societies.

Whether or not you believe in God or in Jesus being who he said he was—the Son of God—or whether you believe that he was simply a great moral teacher (which would be contradictory, if he was a great moral teacher and lied about who he was), the principles he espoused: love God and love

---

[46] Dictionary.com

one another—"love thy neighbor as thyself"[47]—have great, incalculable societal and individual value.

Few would dispute that if there was a pervasive attitude of love of God and of our neighbor, we would deal fairly with each other in intent, word, and action.

Contemplate the following excerpt shared by an ancient prophet about a group of people who lived by this principle of love: "And it came to pass that there was no contention in the land, because of the love of God which did dwell in the hearts of the people."[48]

In order to resolve the problems related to dishonesty in our society, we need to abandon the perception that tougher laws and better enforcement will solve them. There aren't enough police officers or courts to deter dishonest people from committing crimes. We need to address the *root causes,* not the symptoms. Attitudes about dishonesty will not be fixed by law enforcement. That approach is akin to dealing with filthy automobile exhaust rather than fixing the engine and exhaust systems that cause it.

There are no quick fixes. It may take a generation or two to begin to turn things around. A primary solution is in teaching

---

[47] Holy Bible, King James Version 1611, John 13:34
[48] Book of Mormon-4 Nephi v 15

correct principles, beginning in the home, in the churches and schools, and in our work environment.

Holding regular family councils can be an effective way to discuss difficult issues the family is dealing with. This should provide an opportunity to solicit input from all members— even young children. Questions like, "what could we do better as a family?" or "what do we need to do differently?" could result in surprising or even uncomfortable answers. But each person should feel comfortable sharing their feelings— without accusation, and without the threat of being told, "You shouldn't feel that way". The family council could be used as a forum to discuss and teach about honesty, for example.

The same methods can be used to reset a business culture that has become unhealthy or ineffective when a principle-centered approach hasn't been followed. A regularly scheduled company or department meeting to have such a leadership council could pay big dividends. It is what Dr. Stephen R. Covey termed as "Sharpening the Saw", in "The Seven Habits of Highly Effective People". To paraphrase Dr. Covey's analogy, 'we should never become too busy sawing that we can't stop and sharpen the saw.'[49]

The following are ideas and guidelines to consider what to include in such councils:

---

[49] Stephen R. Covey, "The Seven Habits of Highly Effective People", Simon & Schuster, 1989, pp 287-307

Family and business councils

- Start with the big picture, where you are versus where you want to be
- Start fresh—provide a chance to start over
- Set progress goals
- Set ethical behavioral expectations up front
- Set up a reward system
- Evaluate progress
- Require accountability
- Teach correct principles
- Accept responsibility for past harmful behaviors or shortcomings
- Make commitments to practice correct principles—give the why—the vision and end-game goals

Imagine a society like this:

- The U.S. legal code is ¼" thick
- The U.S. tax code is 10 pages—two-sided
- Stores don't experience shoplifting or inventory theft from employees
- All but the most complex deals are done on a handshake
- No one has to lock their doors day or night, locks are optional
- No passwords are required to keep accounts safe
- Prison facilities are turned into housing for the homeless, cell bars are removed
- People don't have to cross their fingers behind their back when making a promise

- Proctors and video cameras are not required for testing centers
- State troopers are almost as bored and lonely as Maytag repairmen
- CEO's tell it like it is. Corporate books are transparent. Accounting is based on GAAP and ethical guidelines

You get the idea. Life would be simpler. We could trust each other. We would make a fair wage or profit.
We would get what we expect and pay for (not in a bad way, either). A person's word would be their bond. We can do it, but we must work together. The incentives for dishonesty must be removed. Perhaps our motives need to be re-examined. Consider the following motives:

- Make or save money, no matter the cost or method, or no matter who is harmed?
- Save face, avoid embarrassment?
- Create a fabricated impression to win a deal, a friend, or an election?
- Avoid punishment even though we are at fault?
- Get something for nothing?

There has to be a concerted effort by enough people to live by tried and true principles and to hold each other accountable. I have to care more about you than I do about me and vice versa. Thankfully, we can find examples of integrity that may guide our attitudes and commitments. A couple of examples follow.

Examples of integrity

The descendants of Fred Snowberger tell with pride the following story of Fred's integrity. The story begins with Fred fulfilling a dream to have his own business. During the depression, in the 1930's, Fred started a pharmacy, but it would be years before the economy would turn around. Eight months into his new venture, and saddled with the debt he had incurred to start his business, he had to close the business. Many told him to declare bankruptcy to end the debt, but Fred ignored their counsel, being determined to repay the entire debt. His honor was more important than having the debt legally expunged.

Fred's family lived frugally, eating what they grew in their garden, making their own clothes, using everything until it was worn out or gone, and Fred walking miles to work every day in fair or inclement weather. This saved the family enough money to allow Fred to make monthly payments on the loan—whatever he could.

After many years of living in this manner, the long-awaited day arrived when Fred would finish paying back the loan. As Fred personally delivered the final payment to his benefactor, the man said, through his tears, "You not only paid back every penny, but you taught me what a man of character and honesty is."[50]

---

[50] Adapted from the Ensign April, 2004 "Earthly Debts, Heavenly Debts" Joseph B. Wirthlin of the Quorum of the Twelve Apostles

Wouldn't it be wonderful if every family had a parent, a grandparent, or great grandparent they could point back to as a shining light of integrity to the current and rising generation? Each of their progenitors could say, in essence, "I belong to his/her family. I'm proud of their legacy. I don't want to do anything to disappoint them or to tarnish their good name." It is amazing how one person's integrity can affect so many. Just imagine if that sort of example could be multiplied by thousands and tens of thousands!

* * *

Multi-million dollar major league pitcher Jeremy Affeldt (San Francisco Giants) followed the path of honor and integrity when he returned $500,000 mistakenly paid to him in 2010 due to a clerical error in preparing his contract. Affeldt obtained multiple opinions that he could legally keep the money, but after talking with his agent, Michael Moye, he determined it would be unethical to keep it. Moye had said, "As a man who represents integrity, I'm saying you should give it back." Affeldt had the contract revised, taking the $500,000 out of it and he returned the money.

Affeldt recounts a conversation he had the next day with General Manager Bobby Evans. "'I can't take that money," Affeldt said. "I won't sleep well at night knowing I took that money because every time I open my paycheck I'll know it's not right." [51]

Perhaps at the end of a long and satisfying career, Jeremy will feel to say, as did Robert Frost, "two roads diverged in a yellow wood . . . I took the one less travelled by, and that has made all the difference." [52]

***

The transformation we seek will require individual and collective effort. One of the key lessons of the book, "The Boys in the Boat" by Daniel James Brown, was each individual unselfishly giving their effort for the good of the team. If they had any hope of winning regional and national rowing races to get the opportunity to compete in the Olympics—not to mention winning their 8-oarsman race in the 1936 Olympics in Nazi Germany—they would have to row precisely and in perfect beautiful harmony. This would mean that they would have to care more about the others in the boat than to seek their own personal aggrandizement. They would have to become, in essence, one organism.

---

[51] "Jeremy Affeldt returns $500,000 to San Francisco Giants after noticing clerical error in contract" by David Brown *May 15, 2013 1:40 PM* Big League Stew (Yahoo Sports)

[52] "The Road Not Taken", Robert Frost

Conclusion

Can we achieve such unity of purpose? Can we move past "looking out for number one" to discover that when we each do our individual civic and moral duty, all will benefit? Can we discern that in the long run, honesty and integrity cost so little when compared to dishonest behaviors in their many forms? We don't have to worry about not having enough. How much is enough anyway? "A rising tide floats all boats". Perhaps we can if we build it one individual, one family or household, one community at a time. It will take concerted effort to "back away from the precipice", to move our society to a place of safety, through honesty and integrity. It can be done, if we work together.

Bibliography

"(The) Adventures of Pinocchio", Carlo Lorenzini (pen name, Carlo Collodi (November 24, 1826 – October 26, 1890)

Al-Hadith, Analysis and an Overview

(The) American Academy of Religion

(The) American Party Battle: election campaign pamphlets

"Book of Mormon, Another Testament of Jesus Christ", LDS Scriptures

Brainyquote.com, copyright 2001-2015 (On-line source for famous quotations)

CBS News

Collected Works of Abraham Lincoln, Volume VI

Dictionary.com (on-line dictionary)

"As good as Our Bond", Sheldon F. Child, Ensign Magazine April 1997

"Earthly Debts, Heavenly Debts", Joseph B. Wirthlin, Ensign Magazine April 2004

Factcheck.org ('consumer advocate' website for voters that aims to reduce the level of deception and confusion in U.S. politics)

Franklin D. Roosevelt, First Inaugural Address

Holy Bible, King James Version, 1611

LA Times (newspaper)

Marketwatch (Online Financial site)

Merriam Webster on-line dictionary

National Association for Shoplifting Prevention

NBC News

New York Times (newspaper)

Notable-quotes.com (On-line source for famous quotations)

Papers of Frederick Douglass, Manuscript Division, Library of Congress

Parshat Toldot by Aryeh Citron

"Principle Centered Leadership", Stephen R. Covey, Simon and Schuster, Inc., 1990, p. 14

Proceedings of the U.S. Naval Institute

Public Broadcasting System (PBS)

Quran (the central religious text of Islam)

Reuters (news service)

Robert Frost, "The Road Not Taken" (poem)

"The Seven Habits of Highly Effective People", Stephen R. Covey, Simon & Schuster, 1989, pp 287-307
Sylvia Boorstein (author)
Wall Street Journal (newspaper)
Walt Disney Pictures, Inc. (film Production Company and division of The Walt Disney Studios, owned by The Walt Disney Company)
Washington Post (newspaper)
Wictionary.com (on-line dictionary)
Wikipedia.com (on-line encyclopedia)
Yahoo Sports, Big League Stew